CHILDREN'S LIT.

PAINE

Looking at Sculpture.

DATE DUE			
3-27-89			
MAR 1 3			
APR 4			

Looking At Sculpture

LOOKING AT

SCULPTURE

Roberta M. Paine

Lothrop, Lee & Shepard Co. ॐ New York

Credits for Sculpture Shown in Front of Book

Moses (detail of head) 1513-16, marble by Michelangelo, on the tomb of Pope Julius II in the Church of San Pietro in Vincoli, Rome, Italy. *Photograph by Anderson*

Striding Lion, glazed brick relief panel from King Nebuchadnezzar's (605-562 B.C.) Processional Way at Babylon, 6th century B.C., 3 feet 2¼ inches high x 7 feet 5½ inches wide. *The Metropolitan Museum of Art, Fletcher Fund, 1931*

Portrait of Peter Vischer, The Elder, bronze replica of figure on the Shrine of St. Sebald at Nuremberg, Germany, by Peter Vischer, The Younger, early 16th century, 15 inches high. *The Metropolitan Museum of Art, The Jules S. Bache Collection, 1949*

Gudea, Sumerian ruler, from Lagash, ca. 2150 B.C., diorite, 17⁵⁄₁₆ inches high. *The Metropolitan Museum of Art, Harris Brisbane Dick Fund, 1959*

For Josephine

Contents

Looking At Sculpture · 10

What is Sculpture? · 13

SCULPTURE IN THE ROUND · 20

Stone · 22

Wood · 44

Clay · 54

Bronze · 62

CONSTRUCTIONS · 72

SCULPTURE IN RELIEF · 82

Map · 100

Notes on the Sculptors · 103

Glossary · 111

Books For Further Reading · 125

Index to Sculpture · 127

Looking At Sculpture

Looking At Sculpture

·IO·

It is fortunate for us that there have always been artists with the skill to carve, model, hammer, and weld. For from that skill, combined with the imagination of the artist, have come such varied forms as these:

The Portrait of a Famous Man

Benjamin Franklin (1706–90), marble portrait head by Jean-Antoine Houdon, 1778, French, 22½ inches high. The Metropolitan Museum of Art, Gift of John Bard, 1872

A Symbol of a Nation

American Eagle, gilded wood by an unknown American sculptor sometime between 1800–30, 62 inches high. The Metropolitan Museum of Art, Ella Morris dePeyster Fund

The Mummy Case
for a Sacred Cat

Mummy Case for a Cat,
bronze made in honor of the
goddess Bastet, with
ancient gold earrings,
Egyptian, late Dynastic to
early Ptolemaic Period, about
900–300 B.C., 15 inches high.
*The Metropolitan Museum of
Art, Funds from various
donors, 1958*

A Pure Shape in Space

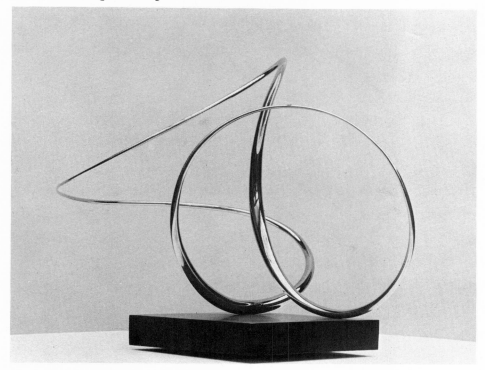

Homage to the World of Minkowski, about 1955, chrome, nickel, and stainless
steel design by José de Rivera, American, 14⅞ inches high, *The Metropolitan
Museum of Art, Fletcher Fund, 1955*

Looking at sculpture in the original is easy since it is all around us. Statues and monuments stand before our public buildings or inside them, and in our cemeteries and parks. Sculpture ornaments our buildings, automobiles, and ships, and even appears on such small familiar objects as our coins.

Taking a closer look at the sculpture that is all around us and at the sculpture preserved in museums, we enter an exciting new world. Here, in a fascinating version, is the whole story of mankind.

The photographs in this book bring together sculpture from many countries and many periods of time. And while pictures and books can never take the place of actual works of art, they do help us discover some of the special characteristics of sculpture. We see how the sculptor designs and carries out his work, and learn something of the materials he uses.

What is Sculpture?

Sculpture is the art of arranging shapes in space. It is three-dimensional art, for all sculpture has length, width, and depth. It can be made from any substance that will hold a shape, but the most usual materials have been some form of stone, wood, clay, or metal. Sculpture may be made in the *round*, to be looked at from all sides, or in *relief*. All sculpture falls into these two groups.

· 13 ·

Sculpture in Relief

Sculpture in the Round

LEFT *Three Quail Chicks,* unfinished limestone relief, Egyptian, about 3rd century B.C., 6 inches high x 5¾ inches wide. *The Metropolitan Museum of Art, Gift of J. Pierpont Morgan, 1911*

RIGHT *Figure of Dignity—Irish Mountain Goat,* 1932, granite with horns of cast aluminum by John Bernard Flannagan, American, 53¾ inches high. *The Metropolitan Museum of Art, Gift of the Alexander Shilling Fund, 1941*

A piece of sculpture is not a mere imitation of a real figure; it represents the artist's concept of people, animals, or shapes of nature. Sculpture is art when it can help us see shapes we have never seen before, and when it shows us something about our world and ourselves in a new way. To achieve this, sculptors are selective; they choose and concentrate on a special characteristic or quality of a figure that interests them. In the five figures of horses we see that each is a special arrangement of the shapes that make up the body of a horse. Each figure is very different, representing a different quality or characteristic of horses in general. It is easy to see which design is concerned with an image of power, of speed, of alertness, of grace, of obedience.

· I4 ·

LEFT *Rearing Horse,* bronze casting from a model by Leonardo da Vinci, Italian, early 16th century, 8½ inches high. *The Metropolitan Museum of Art, Rogers Fund, 1925*

RIGHT *Horse,* bronze, Greek, 8th century B.C., 6 15/16 inches high. *The Metropolitan Museum of Art, Rogers Fund, 1921*

Horse-Shaped Aquamanile, bronze, German, 15th century, 13½ inches high. *The Metropolitan Museum of Art, Gift of William M. Laffan, 1910*

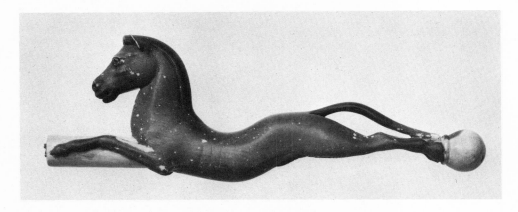

Whip Handle in the shape of a horse, ivory, Egyptian, XVIII Dynasty (1567–1320 B.C.), 6 inches long. *The Metropolitan Museum of Art, Carnarvon Collection, gift of Edward S. Harkness, 1926*

The Horse, 1914, bronze by Raymond Duchamp-Villon, French, 40 inches high. *Collection, The Museum of Modern Art, New York, Van Gogh Purchase Fund*

In sculpture depicting human beings we see an even greater variety of shapes and qualities. This variety is one of the things that makes sculpture so fascinating.

Each of these heads and faces is good sculpture, though each represents a different point of view toward human form.

A face may be idealized. Everything that is uneven or ugly is left out in order to create an image of perfect beauty

Princess Meryetaten, alabaster, Egyptian, XVIII Dynasty, about 1379–62 B.C., 7 inches high. *The Metropolitan Museum of Art, Bequest of Theodore M. Davis, 1930*

A face may be a portrait, a likeness of an individual

President Andrew Jackson (1767–1845), marble portrait bust by Hiram Powers, 1837, American, 34¼ inches high. *The Metropolitan Museum of Art, Gift of Mrs. Frances V. Nash, 1894*

A face may be an exaggeration of physical forms that makes us more aware of the shapes and patterns of human features

Head of a Woman, 1909, bronze by Pablo Picasso, Spanish, 16¼ inches high, *Collection, The Museum of Modern Art, New York, Photograph by Herbert Matter*

*A face may be a
mask, a disguise
for a man which
makes him feel he
has special powers*

African Mask, ivory, made for Bwame secret society, Republic of the Congo,
19th century, 8 inches high. *Courtesy of The Museum of Primitive Art, New
York, Photograph by Charles Uht*

Sleeping Muse, 1909–10, bronze by Constantin Brancusi, Rumanian, 6¾ inches
high x 9½ inches long. *The Metropolitan Museum of Art, The Alfred Stieg-
litz Collection, 1949*

*A face may be
a concentration
on the oval,
the one basic
shape common to
all human heads*

SCULPTURE
IN THE ROUND

Geometric shapes are the basis for all sculpture, as they are for everything else in the world.

A sculptor who creates a figure in the round is very much aware of shape and structure. He knows that everything has a top and a bottom, a front and a back. To him the various sides of a figure are *planes.*

Planes bounded by straight lines and arranged in this way create a cube.

Planes bounded by curved lines and arranged like this make an ovoid, the shape of a human head.

Planes enclose a *volume.* Volume may be space as in a hollow cube, or it may be a solid mass. *Planes, volume, mass,* and *space* are everyday words for sculptors, who look at shapes, and study, analyze, and recreate them as compositions in solid materials.

There is no art form in which material and technique combined play such an important part as they do in sculpture. Each material has its own color, texture, and degree of hardness; each also has its own tools and technical processes. A sculptor selects the material that best suits his design and the final use or location of the sculpture. To appreciate sculpture, we should consider the material used in a particular work as well as its design.

· 21 ·

The Spanish Dance by Edgar Degas, late 19th century, bronze, French, 17 inches high, *The Metropolitan Museum of Art, The H. O. Havemeyer Collection, Bequest 1929*

Stone

Sculpture made from stone is carved; the waste material is cut away with a mallet and chisels. There are many different kinds of stone from which to choose. Some, like alabaster, soapstone, and limestone, are soft and relatively easy to cut. Others, such as granite, hard-grade marble, and diorite, are extremely hard. A sculptor chooses stone for its color and for its grain. If his sculpture is to be placed outdoors, he will probably select a hard stone that is weather resistant.

·23·

Sculptor Carving a Statue, stone relief by Andrea Pisano, about 1340, on the Campanile (Bell Tower) of the Cathedral in Florence, Italy. *Photograph by Alinari*

The ancient Egyptians carved statues of their kings which have lasted for thousands of years. The solemn image of King Amenophis is carved from a dark gray diorite. You can imagine the original shape of the piece of material, for the planes of the figure are as straight as the planes of a square block of stone. The Egyptian sculptor retained the solid mass of his stone. It is heavy, and it *looks* heavy. The statue is a design of perfect balance. If you drew a line down the middle you would see that both halves of the body are exactly alike. This sort of balance is called *symmetry*.

· 24 ·

King Amenophis III (1417–1379 B.C.), dark gray diorite, Egyptian, XVIII Dynasty, 7 feet, 5¾ inches high. *The Metropolitan Museum of Art, Exchange with the Egyptian Government, 1922*

Although most of the Egyptian sculpture we see today has been buried for centuries, it has lasted well. When archaeologists discover broken pieces, they fit them together again and restore them to their original form. In the tombs of Egypt, archaeologists have also discovered some of the ancient sculptors' tools and the models they used, as well as pictures of the sculptors at work. The paintings show us that making a statue of a king was a group project, and also that the tools of carving have changed very little since ancient times.

·26·

Queen Hatshepsut (1503–1482 B.C.) red granite, excavated at Thebes and restored, 28 2/3 inches high. *The Metropolitan Museum of Art, Museum Excavations, 1922–23*

Mallet and Chisel, Egyptian, XI Dynasty (2133–1991 B.C.), *The Metropolitan Museum of Art, Museum Excavations, 1926–27*

Excavations at Thebes, Egypt, 1922–23. In the background on the left is the temple built in honor of Queen Hatshepsut about 1490 B.C. Here archaeologists are sorting pieces of the Queen's statues that they have excavated. Many of the statues, like the one here where the Queen is kneeling with an offering to the gods, were fitted back together again. *Photograph, The Metropolitan Museum of Art.*

The sculptors' models show that they followed guides as they cut into the huge blocks of stone. These guides gave them the proper proportions of a figure. For certainly the face of a king must be perfect! In Egypt, a sculptured royal face was considered ideal if divided into seven facets; three on each side of the face, and one through the nose and center of the chin.

Sculptor's Model of a Royal Head, limestone, about 3rd century B.C., Egyptian, 5¼ inches high. *The Metropolitan Museum of Art, Rogers Fund, 1907*

Egyptian Sculptors at Work, drawing from a tomb painting at Thebes, about 1450 B.C. *The Metropolitan Museum of Art*

Sculpture from light-colored stone makes a livelier, brighter image. Harp Player is carved from a creamy white alabaster. It was found on one of the Cyclades Islands in the Aegean Sea. These islands lie off the east coast of Greece and were first inhabited in prehistoric times. This statuette may look very modern but it is in fact more than 4,000 years old. It is a delightful arrangement of shapes that show us a minstrel who long ago sang songs and told stories of gods and goddesses, heroes and daring deeds. Who made it we do not know, for the early people who lived on the Cyclades are still very much a mystery.

Centuries later these islands were a part of Greece, as they are today. Marble from the Cyclades was brought by ship to the mainland and used for many of the buildings and statues of classical Greece.

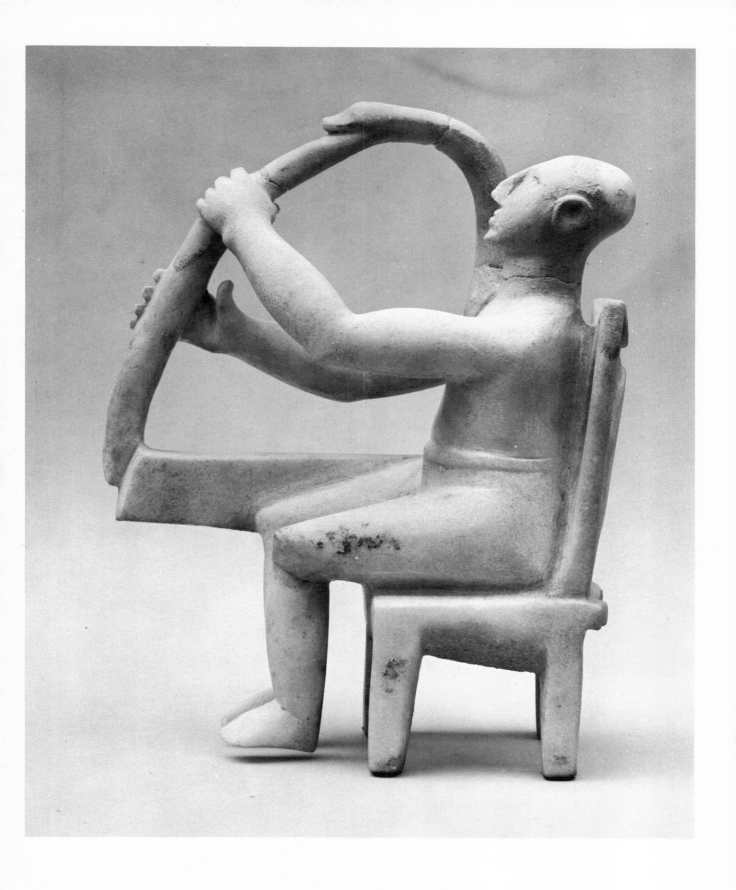

Harp Player, translucent marble, about 2500 B.C., from the Cyclades Islands, 11½ inches high. *The Metropolitan Museum of Art, Rogers Fund, 1947*

Greek sculptors introduced something new to art in the ancient world. They were the first to carve statues that capture the natural forms and movements of human beings. We call this *naturalism*.

Many have tried to imitate Greek sculpture and have failed, for Greek sculpture is not simply a skillful copying of human anatomy as in wax museum figures. Like all good sculpture, it is essentially a design, emphasizing particular qualities.

The six statues of Maidens on the Erectheum in Athens are figures of dignity, poise, and strength. The artists responsible for this sculpture designed it to express certain qualities, and they also had in mind its placement as columns for a building. We see the Maidens as natural in form, yet each with a special pose and surface carving that keeps it from being merely "lifelike." One leg of each figure is straight, and the other bent. The straight leg is a cylinder, the surface cut with vertical lines. The cylindrical shape is that of an ordinary column, while the lines resemble the flutings or grooves on a column. In this kind of arrangement, the statues *look* strong enough to hold up a roof of stone, as they in fact do. (See page 34.)

·32·

Six Maidens, marble caryatid figures on the Porch of the Erectheum, a temple on the Acropolis in Athens, Greece, built 421 B.C.; each figure is 6 feet 7 inches high. *Photograph by Alinari*

Close-Up View of the Porch of the Maidens. Photograph by Alinari

The Greeks used sculpture in many ways. Some statues were monuments to important people or events. The Victory of Samothrace was a war memorial. It commemorated a naval battle off the coast of the island of Samothrace. There on the island a statue in the form of a goddess was erected. She is poised as if on the prow of a ship. Since earliest times the Greeks had been interested in movement. The Victory expresses body movement as well as the movement of wind. The sweeping curves suggest that the goddess is pressed against a strong wind.

Victory of Samothrace, marble by Greek sculptors from Rhodes about 190 B.C., 8 feet high. *The Museé de Louvre, Paris. Photograph by Alinari*

Sculpture that is natural in form and also emphasizes strong human emotions, particularly painful and unpleasant ones like anger or despair, we call *realistic*. The Laocoön is realistic sculpture. It illustrates a moment recorded in Greek history and myth that represents agony, struggle, and certain death. During the Trojan War, the Greeks left their fabled wooden horse outside the city of Troy and pretended to sail for home. Laocoön, a Trojan priest, suspected a trick and warned his fellow Trojans to beware of Greeks bearing gifts. No one believed his warning, or guessed that the horse was hollow and concealed Greek soldiers waiting to make a surprise attack. Athena, the goddess who helped the Greeks, was afraid of Laocoön's wisdom, so she sent two huge serpents up from the sea to kill him and his two sons.

The horrifying moment of the serpents' attack is the subject of the sculpture. It is easy to be distracted by the details of writhing bodies and coiling snakes and not notice that the group does have an over-all design; it is a geometric shape—a pyramid.

Laocoön was once in the art collection of the Roman Emperor Titus (A.D. 40-81). Then sometime after the fall of the Roman Empire, the sculpture was lost, or so it seemed. One day in 1506, workmen were clearing out old stones from a vineyard in Rome. There in the rubble and dirt they found Laocoön. It was an exciting moment; city officials, even the Pope, Julius II, came to see the ancient sculpture. The Pope claimed it for his own art collection and it has been in the Vatican ever since. Artists came to see Laocoön too, among them Michelangelo Buonarroti.

Laocoön and His Sons, marble group from the workshop of Hagesandros, Anthanodoros, and Polydoros of Rhodes, Greek, about 50–25 B.C., 8 feet high. *The Vatican Museum, Rome. Photograph by Anderson*

Michelangelo, in 1506, was already a famous and successful artist, even though he did grumble a good deal about not being properly appreciated. One of his patrons was Pope Julius for whom he painted the ceiling of the Sistine Chapel. Michelangelo was an artist of many talents, but his first love was sculpture. He is credited with saying that within every block of stone there is a figure waiting to be set free. These words perfectly describe his unfinished carving called Atlas.

One of Michelangelo's major commissions was to design and carve sculpture for Pope Julius' tomb. This project was stopped and started several times by the Pope, much to Michelangelo's disappointment. He never completed the work, but what he did has made the tomb famous; his Moses is one of the best-known statues in the world. It is an artist's image of a noble man, and suggests deep thought and purpose. Though Moses is seated, we see him as restless and a man of action. The head is turned; the left leg is drawn back; the folds of the robe are arranged in sweeping curves; the beard is a pattern of wavy curls. Yet all this restless movement and the details of muscular strength are kept within the space limit of the block of stone from which the figure was carved.

"Atlas" or Prisoner Figure, one of the four unfinished marble statues for the Tomb of Pope Julius II, between 1530–33, 9 feet 1½ inches high. *The Galleria dell' Accademia, Florence, Italy. Photograph by Alinari*

Moses, 1513–16, marble figure in a niche on the tomb of Pope Julius II in the Church of San Pietro in Vincoli (St. Peter in Chains), Rome, Italy, 8 feet 3½ inches high. *Photograph by Anderson*

The horns on the head of Moses are a symbol and a tradition in art that depicts this Bible figure. An early mistranslation of a passage in the Book of Exodus described Moses as coming down from Mt. Sinai with rays of light radiating from his head. The word for *rays* was translated as *horns.*

Guardian Figure, limestone from Castillo de Teayo, Veracruz, Mexico, Aztec, about 1480–91, 31⅝ inches high. *The Metropolitan Museum of Art, Dick Fund, 1962*

Pyramid Temple at Tulum, Mexico, lithograph from a watercolor drawing by Frederick Catherwood (1799–1854), British. Guardian figures were made to sit on either side of the top step of pyramids like this. Drawing published, London, 1844; in the New York Public Library.

Since earliest times the human figure has been the sculptor's greatest challenge. Men, women, and children appear in sculpture more often than any other subject. Not all works portraying human beings as subject matter show us kings, queens, superhuman beings, or prophets though. We see the ordinary people too. The guardian figure for an Aztec temple in ancient Mexico is perfectly shaped to stand at the top step of a sacred pyramid. In the solid geometric shape, a sculptor created a design that shows us a common man, patient and obedient to the will of his overlords.

·41·

In the twentieth century sculptors have found new ways to show us man—not a particular man or a particular type of man but all men. For the human figure may be portrayed as pure design, a design that includes the essential shapes that make up all human forms. Kouros (young man) is what we call an *abstraction*. It leaves out all the familiar surface details of human beings and concentrates on the basic shapes, the very bone structure. Abstract sculpture gives us still another view of people.

·42·

Kouros, 1944–45, marble by Isamu Noguchi, American, 9 feet 9 inches high. *The Metropolitan Museum of Art, Fletcher Fund, 1953*

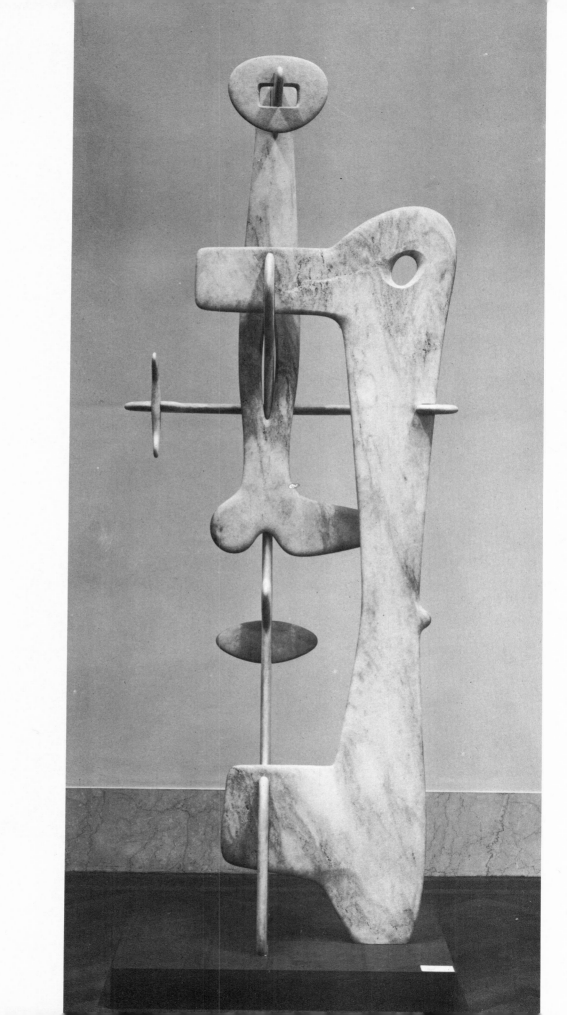

Wood

Sculptor Carving a Corinthian Capital, painted wood, French, 18th century, 14½ inches high. Here a sculptor works with mallet and gouge. *The Metropolitan Museum of Art, Gift of J. Pierpont Morgan, 1906*

Wood has been used for sculpture for centuries, but comparatively little has survived from ancient times. When it is neglected it will rot, crack, or become infested with worms. Wooden sculpture has been found well preserved in Egypt where it had been placed in tombs which remained dry and airtight. Not only painted statues of kings and gods were made of wood but also models of servants engaged in their everyday duties, as shown on page 47, and carved mummy cases of their employers.

Egyptian Mummy Cases, painted wooden coffins of Khonsu, XX Dynasty (1200–1085 B.C.), 6 feet high. *The Metropolitan Museum of Art, Purchase, 1886*

Wood is easier to carve than stone, although it requires very sharp tools to cut through the woody fibers. Axes and saws are used to take off the first waste material. Gouges and chisels are used for the carving and cutting of the outline and details of a figure. Sandpaper is used for smoothing the surface. A most important step in working in wood is the *seasoning*. Wood must be dried out after it is cut from a tree. Some sculptors say that, for best results, a piece of wood should be allowed to dry for a number of years. This is the opposite of stone, which is considered best when it is used freshly cut from a quarry.

Ancient Model of Boat from the tomb of Meket-re at Thebes, Egypt, painted wood, XI Dynasty, about 2000 B.C., length about 41 inches. *The Metropolitan Museum of Art, Museum Excavations, 1920*

A sculptor may select a piece of wood and design a figure in the round that closely follows the original shape of the log. Both Lillian Leitzel and the Chinese Man retain the round, cylinder shapes of the logs of wood from which each was carved. On the other hand, wood can offer a sculptor great freedom of design, for he may join pieces of wood together.

Tomb Figure, painted wood from Ch'ang-Sha, Chinese, Late Chou Dynasty, about 5th to 3rd century B.C., 23¼ inches high. *The Metropolitan Museum of Art, Gift of Mathias Konor, 1948*

LEFT *Lillian Leitzel* (1894–1931), macassar ebony by Chaim Gross, 1938, American, 52 inches high. *The Metropolitan Museum of Art, Rogers Fund, 1942*

Kuan Yin, Buddhist Goddess of Mercy, painted wood, Chinese, Late Sung Dynasty (960–1279), 46½ inches high. *The Metropolitan Museum of Art, Fletcher Fund, 1928*

The Chinese sculpture of Kuan Yin is pieced and doweled. The joinings are so tight and smooth they do not show. By piecing the wood the sculptor designed Kuan Yin with arms that stretch out into the surrounding space. The result is a figure that expresses a grace and elegance very suitable for the Buddhist Goddess of Mercy.

Most wood is easier to cut than stone, so we find many sculptors selecting wood when their design calls for surface decorations. The hair, clothing, jewelry, of Kuan Yin—each is a different pattern against the smooth skin areas. All sculpture may be painted, and on soft woods, painting serves as protection as well as decoration. The thirteenth-century Virgin and Child is of painted wood. Although it is 700 years old, the original flesh tones and the reds and blues of the clothing are still bright. It is a pleasing and natural design made for a medieval church in France.

·51·

Virgin and Child, painted wood, French, late 13th century, 15⅞ inches high. *The Metropolitan Museum of Art, Gift of J. Pierpont Morgan, 1917*

Harpsichord, gilded wood relief illustrating the procession of the goddess Galatea; large statues of Polyphemus and Galatea, Italian, 17th century, 8½ feet long. *The Metropolitan Museum of Art, The Crosby Brown Musical Instrument Collection, 1889*

Wood has been used in many ways to decorate the things we use, for example musical instruments. Many of these are made from wood because this is the material best suited to produce resonant sounds. The Indians of the American Northwest carved designs on the surface of their wooden ceremonial rattles; while sculptors of Europe enriched the surface of a harpsichord and added *freestanding* sculpture in the round.

Northwest American Indian Rattle, wood, 11½ inches high. *The Metropolitan Museum of Art, The Crosby Brown Musical Instrument Collection, 1889*

There is probably no wood sculpture of greater interest to Americans than the graceful figureheads that once graced the bows of the nineteenth-century sailing ships. The figureheads of ships were a means of identification as well as splendid decorations. The old wooden ships are gone now, but many of the figureheads were removed and saved. They remain carefully protected as sculpture in museums.

Figurehead, painted wood about 1805, attributed to Samuel McIntire, American, 26 inches high. *The Peabody Museum, Salem, Massachusetts*

Figurehead and Bow of the *Great Admiral Ship,* built in 1869 at Boston, Massachusetts. *Photograph courtesy of The Peabody Museum, Salem, Massachusetts*

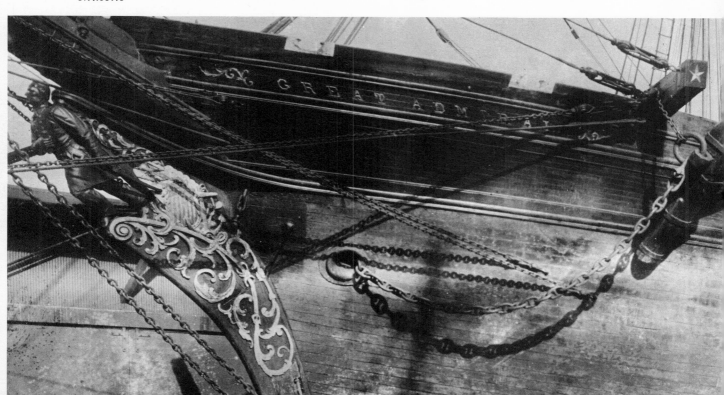

Clay

The Sculptor, Carl Milles at work in his studio in Rome, about 1952. He is modeling in clay; the figures for the Fountain of Aganippe were cast in bronze for The Metropolitan Museum of Art.

Female Statuette, painted earthenware from Hacilar, Anatolia (now Turkey), about 5400 B.C., 5½ inches high. *The Metropolitan Museum of Art, Gift of H. Dunscombe Colt, 1964*

Clay may be the oldest material for sculpture in the round. Who can tell when a man first picked up some clay or mud and squeezed it into a shape that pleased him? It is such an easy and natural thing to do. It does not require training, special tools, or experience. Only the fingers are needed. For sculpture made from clay is not cut or carved, but modeled. Anyone who has ever modeled a snowman or sandcastle, made a mud pie or a clay object of any sort, knows the pleasure of getting one's hands into a modeling material and watching it take shape.

The oldest piece of sculpture in this book is made of clay. It is the small figure of a woman decorated with painted stripes. In many ancient civilizations clay figures were made for tombs. The small Ox and Cart, and the spirited Horse, are sculptures from clay found in Chinese tombs. Each is a symbol of wealth and usefulness for the dead.

· 55 ·

Ox and Cart, pottery tomb figure, Chinese, T'ang Dynasty (618–906), 17¾ inches long. *The Metropolitan Museum of Art, John Stewart Kennedy Fund, 1913*

Horse, painted pottery tomb figure, Chinese, T'ang Dynasty (618–906), 28 inches high. *The Metropolitan Museum of Art, Rogers Fund, 1925*

Benjamin Franklin and King Louis XVI, porcelain, Niderviller type, French, 1780–85, 12¾ inches high. *The Metropolitan Museum of Art, Gift of William Henry Huntington, 1883*

In later periods figurines of clay have been made to commemorate special events. King Louis XVI and Benjamin Franklin illustrates the signing of the treaty that brought French aid for the American Revolution in 1778. These French figurines were popular with Americans and sold very well.

Clay is an imperishable material when it has been fired, or baked in a kiln. It will not disintegrate with age, but has one serious disadvantage. Masses of clay are very heavy, and will break if not properly supported. Clay can be modeled successfully for large pieces of sculpture in relief which you will see in a later section but is rarely used for large, *permanent* figures in the round.

The exception is clay or plaster used for making large, *temporary* figures. During the eighteenth and nineteenth centuries in both Europe and America it was more often than not the custom of successful and busy sculptors to model a figure from clay and then turn over the cutting of a statue in stone to professional stonecutters.

Triton and Nereid, unpainted terra-cotta sketch by Auguste Rodin, about 1893, French, 16 inches high. *The Metropolitan Museum of Art, Rogers Fund, 1912*

The stonecutters worked by a system called *pointing*. In one room of the *workshop* you can see a full-size figure of clay at the left. It is covered with black *points*, nailheads driven into the surface of the clay. On the partially roughed out stone on the left, the craftsmen have carefully measured and have placed marks that correspond exactly to the points on the clay model. These marks will be guidelines for the stonecutter whose job is to copy faithfully the original clay design. In the second room of the shop, workers are hoisting a block of stone into position. A second clay model waits to be pointed.

All of the sculpture you saw in the section on stone was carved by the *direct method;* the artist carved the stone. Sculpture carved from pointing is called the *indirect method*.

It may seem that clay and other modeling materials like plaster and wax are not very important to the story of sculpture. Nothing could be further from the truth. For not only is clay a sketching material for sculptors; it is the basis for all sculpture cast from bronze.

Two Views of a Stonecutter's Workshop, Pointing Statues, 18th-century French engravings from Diderot's *Encyclopedie ou dictionaire raisonné des sciences* in The Metropolitan Museum of Art.

Bronze

Portrait of Peter Vischer, The Elder, bronze replica of figure on the Shrine of St. Sebald at Nuremberg, Germany, by Peter Vischer, The Younger, early 16th century, 15 inches high. The artist showed his father wearing a round cap, leather apron, and holding the tools of his trade: a metal hammer and point. *The Metropolitan Museum of Art, The Jules S. Bache Collection, 1949*

When bronze was discovered by ancient man, it brought such a change to civilization that the time is called the Bronze Age. Bronze is an alloy of copper and tin. The first bronze was used for tools, weapons, utensils, and armor. But soon man found it a desirable and beautiful material for sculpture. It is strong, withstands weather well, and when cast hollow, is lighter than stone.

·63·

Greek Helmet, bronze, late 7th–early 6th century B.C., 8⅞ inches high. *The Metropolitan Museum of Art, Rogers Fund, 1919*

Athena Flying Her Owl, bronze statuette about 460 B.C., Greek, 5⅞ inches high. *The Metropolitan Museum of Art, Dick Fund, 1950*

Statuettes, or small sculptures like the ancient Greek figure of Athena Flying Her Owl, are cast solid. The process is not too difficult. The sculptor modeled the figure in wax, then covered it with a mixture of clay and sand. When this covering was thoroughly dry, an opening was made at one end and the whole piece heated until all the wax melted away and ran out of the hole. Molten, liquid bronze was then poured in, which took the place previously occupied by the wax. After hours of cooling, the bronze hardened. The outer clay covering was broken off and the figure was complete, ready to be polished.

The Greeks liked to show artists at work, and even more to show a goddess acting as a sculptor. In the picture from a greek vase, Athena is modeling the figure of a horse from clay. She is building up the figure over a frame called an *armature*. The pile of clay lies at her feet. When the clay model is complete, the horse might be cast by the same method used for her statue, cast solid, *or* it might be cast by the *lost wax* process.

Athena Modeling a Horse, drawing from an Athenian vase, Greek, about 460 B.C., in the Berlin Museum, Germany.

Greek artists considered the goddess Athena their special deity and so it was most appropriate for a painter to show her modeling a statue. The tools on the wall are carpenter's tools and would have been used to make the wooden armature, the frame on which the goddess is modeling her horse.

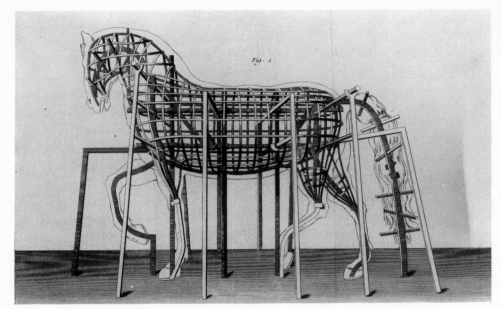

Armature made from wood, wire, and piping for a French, 18th-century equestrian sculpture of King Louis XIV, engraving in Diderot's *Encyclopedie ou dictionaire raisonné des sciences* in The Metropolitan Museum of Art.

Casting a Bronze Statue, 18th-century French engravings from Diderot's *Encyclopedie* in The Metropolitan Museum of Art.

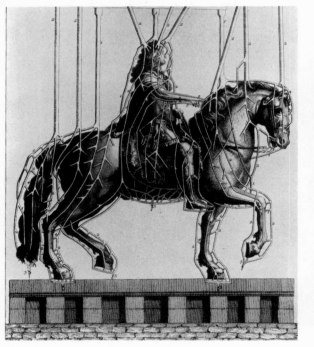

LEFT   Here the figure of king and horse have been made in wax, and the wax rods and channels have been added preparatory to placing the figure in a furnace at the foundry.

RIGHT   The statue of the King is modeled in clay over its armature. Then blocks of plaster are built up around the clay figure. The moist plaster takes the "image" of the clay. This picture shows the model of Louis XIV's statue being piece-molded.

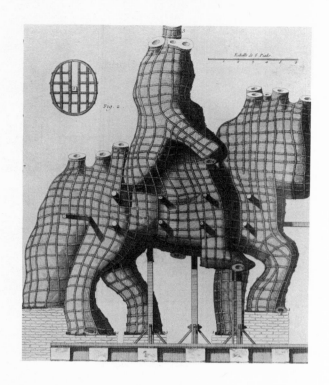

Last, a fire-resistant "overcoat" is put around the figure and held on with iron bands. The equestrian figure is ready to be placed in the casting furnace and receive the liquid bronze through the vent holes.

The lost wax (*cire perdue*) method produces a statue or figure that is hollow. Therefore it is very suitable for large pieces, since it saves material and makes a lighter statue. To cast a hollow figure requires additional steps. A core of plaster or clay is surrounded with a layer of wax; the wax is shaped as the sculpture is to look. The wax must be of the same thickness that the final bronze is to be. Hollow wax rods are applied to the surface of the figure. These will act as drainpipes. Now the figure is covered with an outer plaster overcoat and heated as in solid casting. The wax runs out; bronze is poured in; it hardens and the outer covering is removed. The drainpipes are broken off and the interior core of plaster is broken up and shaken out. The surface is polished and burnished.

Casting bronze sculpture is usually left to skilled foundrymen. While it *is* a kind of reproduction, it is an exact and faithful translation of an artist's work in clay or wax into metal. Bronze is such a fluid metal that it can capture every thumb print, every curve an artist models in clay. For sculptors who prefer to model, bronze casting is the technique for preserving their work and making it permanent.

Auguste Rodin was the most celebrated sculptor of the late nineteenth century. His most famous sculpture is the Thinker. Rodin modeled it first in clay and then had it cast in bronze. Since a bronze mold can be used more than once there are several copies of it. Thinker is the image of a giant-man, a figure that focuses our attention on powerful muscles and deep thought. The strain of the muscles, the tension of the body, creates the impression of "thinking." Rodin posed the figure to emphasize strain. The giant rests his right elbow on his left knee. This is not natural—it is in fact most uncomfortable—but the twist and turn it gives to Thinker is just right for the theme of the sculpture.

·69·

The Thinker (Le Penseur), modeled in 1880; cast in bronze in 1910; by Auguste Rodin, French, 27⅝ inches high. *The Metropolitan Museum of Art, Gift of Thomas F. Ryan, 1911*

The bronze illustrated here is made after the plaster figure designed by Rodin for an elaborate gateway to be called the Gate of Hell after Dante's Inferno. The 27-inch-high figure was to be centered above the doorway. The Gate was never completed. Rodin enlarged his small figure of The Thinker to colossal size (6 feet 6 inches high; twice life-size for a seated figure). It was exhibited in Paris in 1904. As more than one bronze can be cast from a mold, there are several bronze versions of this famous statue in both the small and colossal sizes.

Family Group, 1945–49, cast in bronze in 1950, by Henry Moore, British, 59¼ inches high. *Collection, The Museum of Modern Art, New York, A. Conger Goodyear Fund*

Henry Moore's sculpture is as calm in mood as Rodin's is tense. His Family Group is a design of large round forms, gracefully joined by the curving lines of the arms of mother and father. The surface of the sculpture is very smooth. This texture creates a mood of serenity. Bronze is so fluid that it can capture any surface texture desired by a sculptor.

The bold, curving planes that thrust out into space are perfectly cast in the bronze figure Unique Forms. These sweeping forms are symbols of speed and movement. It seems to represent speed in our time, for we know that at supersonic speeds a solid figure can be distorted and even break up. The remarkable thing about this sculpture is that it was made in 1913. Umberto Boccioni was a prophet of things to come.

·71·

Unique Forms of Continuity in Space, 1913, bronze by Umberto Boccioni, Italian, 43½ inches high. *Collection, The Museum of Modern Art, New York, The Lillie P. Bliss Bequest*

CONSTRUCTIONS

An Armorer's Workshop by Hans Burgkmair (1473–1531), German, woodcut
from *Der Weisskunig* in The Metropolitan Museum of Art

What can you pound and bend; cut, weld, rivet, and link? Metal!

In the Middle Ages, armorers cut and shaped pieces of steel for suits of armor. The separate pieces were riveted together and assembled into suits of such excellent design that they can be called sculpture.

The assembling of pieces of metal, building up a design, is still another way to design figures in space. Today the artists who create sculpture from individual pieces of metal or plastic are called *constructionists*. Their works are *constructions*. While the technique of fastening metals together is not new, the designs and ideas of the modern constructionists have added exciting new forms to the story of sculpture.

·73·

Suit of Armor, steel, German, about 1510. *The Metropolitan Museum of Art, Rogers Fund, 1904*

Red Gongs, a mobile made from sheet aluminum, sheet brass, steel rods, wire, and red paint, by Alexander Calder, 20th century, American, about 12 feet long. *The Metropolitan Museum of Art, Fletcher Fund, 1955*

Mobiles are probably the best-known and most imitated constructions. They were invented—both the word and the form—by the American artist Alexander Calder. Red Gongs is assembled from pieces of sheet aluminum, painted red, and from brass and steel rods. The geometric shapes are soldered to the wires, which are hinged with metal links. With a breeze, a mobile turns and swings freely in space. It does not imitate, but it does resemble the motion of leaves, twigs, and light branches of a tree moving in nature. Mobiles are delightful to watch.

Museum Visitors Looking at a Mobile by Alexander Calder in the Junior Museum's special exhibition, How to Look at Sculpture, 1960–62, The Metropolitan Museum of Art.

In contrast to a mobile, Tanktotem is weighty and awesome. It is made from a solid disk of cast bronze and pieces of steel. David Smith, the sculptor, worked in a tank factory during World War II. After the war, he designed sculpture he called totems of modern civilization. He saw the army tank as a totem for twentieth-century people.

·76·

Tanktotem II (Sounding), steel and cast bronze, by David Smith, 1952–53, American, 6 feet 8½ inches high. *The Metropolitan Museum of Art, Fletcher Fund, 1953*

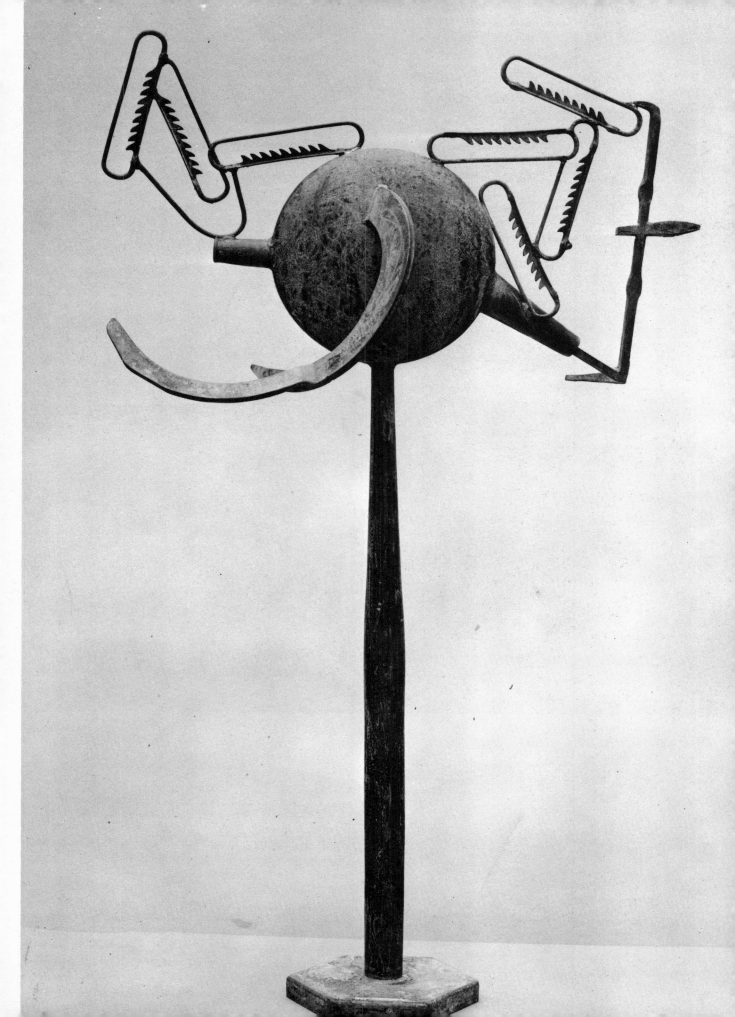

Variation Within a Sphere, No. 10: The Sun, 1953–56, 22k gold-filled wire, by Richard Lippold, American, 11 feet high x 22 feet wide. *The Metropolitan Museum of Art, Fletcher Fund, 1956*

Sun is a construction of golden wires. Richard Lippold used nearly two miles of wire to create this shimmering design expressive of sun and light. He made sketches to plan the design and sketches to show how it should be hung. A central sphere rotates, while radiating planes made up of "rays" are held out taut with guy wires. Sun has all the geometry and ingenuity of a spider web or snow crystal. It is a design of light.

·79·

Pencil and Ink Sketch for "The Sun" by Richard Lippold. *The Metropolitan Museum of Art, Gift of Robert Beverly Hale, 1960*

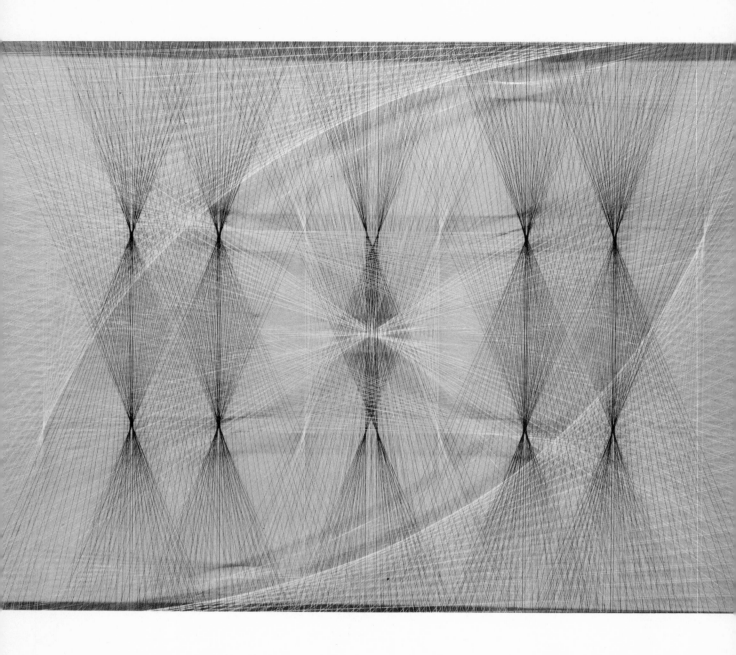

String Composition No. 50, plastic threads against a painted masonite board, by Sue Fuller, 20th-century American, 34 inches high x 45 inches wide. *The Metropolitan Museum of Art, Francis Lathrop Bequest Fund, 1955*

Sue Fuller's Composition is made from plastic threads in a construction that is both mathematical and artistic. The threads are set against a painted board, which is framed like a picture. Therefore it has but one viewing point. It is meant to be seen from the front. This one point of view is the special characteristic of the sculpture called relief.

·8I·

SCULPTURE IN RELIEF

Relief is an art form that is midway between painting and sculpture in the round. It resembles a painting in being a picture or a pattern on a flat surface, but it is also sculpture, for it has three dimensions. All of the materials of sculpture are used for relief. It may be carved from stone or wood, modeled from clay, cast, or beaten from metal.

Sculptors and Stonecutters, stone relief by Nanni di Banco, about 1415, for the base of his sculpture group of four saints on the façade of Or San Michele, Florence, Italy. *Photograph by Alinari.*

Procession of the Emperor and His Courtiers, black marble relief from Pin-Yang Tung (Cave III) at Lung Mèn, Chinese, Northern Wei Dynasty (386–557), 6 feet 10 inches high x 12 feet 11 inches wide. *The Metropolitan Museum of Art, Fletcher Fund, 1935*

Relief may be made in several levels. Each describes the depth or the height of its projection from a flat surface. Looking at sculpture in relief, you will see that it may be in *low relief, high relief, sunk relief,* or *intaglio relief.*

High Relief

Hindu God Vishnu, stone temple relief, Indian (Mysore region), early 12th century, 5 feet 1 inch high x 28 inches wide. *The Metropolitan Museum of Art, Rogers Fund, 1918*

Sunk Relief

Head of King Akhenaten (1379–62 B.C.) from Tell el Amarna, Egypt, XVIII Dynasty, about 1370 B.C., limestone relief made as a sculptor's model or trial piece, 13⅜ inches high x 9 3/16 inches wide. *The Metropolitan Museum of Art, Fletcher Fund and The Guide Foundation, Inc., Gift, 1966*

Intaglio Relief

Stamp Seal, white enameled steatite from the Punjab (now Pakistan), Indian, about 2500 B.C., 1½ inches square. *The Metropolitan Museum of Art, Dodge Fund, 1949*

LEFT *Silver Coin* of 10 Drachmae with the head of the Nymph Arethusa, Greek from Syracuse (Sicily), about 412 B.C., diameter 1 2/5 inches. *The Metropolitan Museum of Art, Gift of J. Pierpont Morgan, 1905*

RIGHT *United States Dime*, 1945, silver and alloys, diameter ¾ inch.

The designs on coins and the designation of value, country, and date of issue are a form of sculpture in low relief. They are certainly the most common and the most easily available sculpture for us to see and to handle.

Stamp seals and signet rings are decorated in relief to establish personal identity. These designs are usually intaglio, that is, cut in reverse into the surface of a stone. When a seal is pressed into clay or wax, the impression will appear correctly. The ancient Indian stamp seal on page 85 is carved with the picture of an ox and some writing. It is thought that the writing is someone's name, but it has not yet been deciphered and remains a mystery.

Many reliefs have been made from clay, which is not ordinarily long-lasting. Little harm can come to a clay relief when its weight is framed or supported by a wall. In the pictures are three clay reliefs which were once the decorations for buildings.

The Striding Lion is modeled on the surface of individual building bricks and comes from the palace of King Nebuchadnezzar of Babylon. The bricks are shaped and modeled in low relief and painted with ceramic glazes. The lion's body is yellow, the mane brown, and the background a turquoise blue.

·87·

Striding Lion, glazed brick relief panel from King Nebuchadnezzar's (605–562 B.C.) Processional Way at Babylon, 6th century B.C., 3 feet 2¼ inches high x 7 feet 5½ inches wide. *The Metropolitan Museum of Art, Fletcher Fund, 1931*

Archangel Saint Michael, glazed terra-cotta, by Andrea della Robbia, about 1475, 5 feet 1⅞ inches high. *The Metropolitan Museum of Art, Dick Fund, 1960*

·88· The Archangel Michael is weighing souls in heaven. The relief is shaped in a lunette, and was made to go over the doorway of a church in Florence, Italy. Like the Lion, this sculpture is glazed. The light parts are white and the background is blue.

This masklike face was modeled from clay as a decoration on the roof of a Greek temple. The "lady" is a Gorgon, one of the snake-haired sisters of Medusa who it was believed turned to stone anyone who looked at her face.

Gorgon Face, painted terra-cotta antefix found at Taranto (Italy), about 540 B.C., little of the paint remains, 8¼ inches high x 10 3/16 inches wide. *The Metropolitan Museum of Art, Dick Fund, 1939*

Carved Wall From a Jaina Temple (detail), teakwood, Indian, about 1594. The Jaina religion is an offshoot from Hinduism and one of the important religious groups of India. *The Metropolitan Museum of Art, Gift of Robert W. and Lockwood De Forest, 1916*

Wood is a splendid material to decorate the interior walls of buildings. There it is protected from the weather. The surfaces of Indian temple walls are often richly and deeply carved in relief. The design is so exuberant that it seems almost to move!

The fine wood paneling and carving of eighteenth-century American homes and public buildings are examples of sculpture in relief. Usually this carving was done by the artist-craftsmen called cabinet-makers, but they, like the sculptors, were artists in the shaping and designing of wood for the decoration of walls and furniture.

· 91 ·

Assembly Room (Ballroom) from the City Tavern at Alexandria, Virginia, built and decorated with carved wood paneling in 1793. On February 22, 1798, George Washington's Birthday Ball was held in this room; it is now in the American Wing of The Metropolitan Museum of Art. *Rogers Fund, 1917*

Town Hall at Seville, Spain, 16th century. Photograph, *The Metropolitan Museum of Art.*

Stone sculpture often decorates the exterior walls of buildings. One of the most elaborate styles was created in Spain during the sixteenth century. The Town Hall in Seville is richly decorated with sculpture in relief.

The mammoth winged lion with a matching bull once guarded the entrance to the palace of a king of ancient Assyria. The lion is a symbol of power, and he is a most unusual example of sculpture in relief. If we look at the lion from the front, he is standing; if we look at him from the side, he is walking! There are really two reliefs here. The sculptor gave the lion five legs, so that two would be seen from the front and four from the side!

Assyrian Winged Lion, stone relief from the palace of King Ashurnasirpal II at Nimrud (in modern Iraq), 9th century B.C., 10 feet 2½ inches high. *The Metropolitan Museum of Art, Gift of John D. Rockefeller, Jr., 1932*

Gold Diadem (Crown), hammered decorations and figures of the god Dionysus and the Princess Ariadne, daughter of King Minos of Crete, Greek, 2⅜ inches high x 14½ inches long, center portion shown here. *The Metropolitan Museum of Art, Rogers Fund, 1906*

Reliefs may be made from precious materials like gold, silver, and ivory. *Repoussé* (thrust back) is a technique used for decorating gold and silver in relief patterns. The design is drawn on the outside of the metal, but beaten out with hammers from the reverse side. The golden headdress is decorated with the figures of the god Dionysus and the princess Ariadne. Because gold is so expensive, sculpture of this kind is usually made on a small scale. Of course there are always exceptions, such as the Sun, mentioned earlier, a construction of golden wires that is eleven feet high.

·94·

Ivory is a beautiful and delicate material which is also expensive, since true ivory comes only from the tusks of elephants. Ivory carving was especially fine during the Middle Ages. Sculpture cut pictures in amazing detail for wealthy kings and nobles. A favorite form was the small altarpiece or *diptych*. This one is cut in high relief with scenes that illustrate the Passion of Christ.

Ivory Diptych with carved scenes of the Passion of Christ, French, 14th century, 8 inches high x 7 inches wide. *The Metropolitan Museum of Art, Rogers Fund, 1950*

Early American Tombstones with sunk and incised relief pictures and inscriptions in the graveyard, The Burying Point, Salem, Massachusetts. *Photograph by the author*

Because man has always wanted to leave behind him a record of himself, the skill and art of sculptors have been called on in every period of time, including our own, to make grave markers and tombs. The rich and the mighty could enlist the services of a Michelangelo. Others might have only the services of a humble stonecutter. But simple or heroic, some of the finest sculpture in relief was made for tombs.

The high relief sculpture of a knight in chain armor is the image of a man who lived and fought in the Middle Ages.

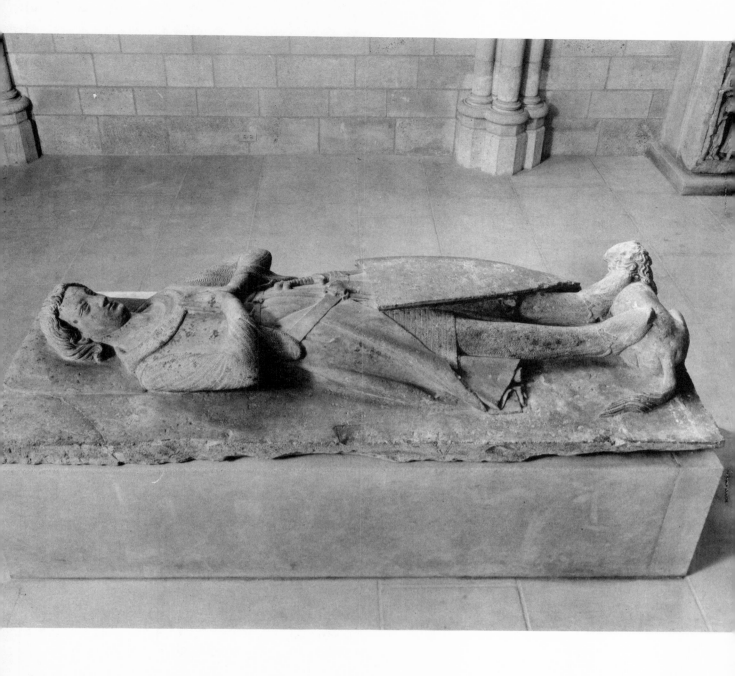

Effigy Figure of a Knight, Jean D'Alluye (d. about 1248) on his tombstone, French, 13th century, 6 feet 11½ inches long x 34¼ inches wide. *The Metropolitan Museum of Art, The Cloisters, Purchase, 1925*

The low relief picture of an ancient Greek warrior stepping into his chariot is on the stone that marked his grave.

Memorials such as these are a part of the continuing story of sculpture—a story with no ending. For whether it be a memorial, a monument, or a miniature, sculpture is all about us, offering pleasure and challenge to all who will look. Through sculpture we often enter into the past, and sometimes, because of the creative imagination of sculptors, we also reach into the future.

Greek Warrior, sunk and low relief marble carving on a grave stele, Greek, 535–25 B.C., size of this relief 13½ inches high x 19¾ inches wide, originally painted, traces of red, black, blue, and green can still be seen. *The Metropolitan Museum of Art, Fletcher Fund, 1938*

ARCTIC OCEAN

PACIFIC
OCEAN

CANADA

NORTH AMERICA

UNITED STATES

ATLANTIC
OCEAN

MEXICO

CENTRAL AMERICA

GULF OF
MEXICO

CARIBBEAN SEA

SOUTH
AMERICA

1. Alexandria, Virginia
2. Athens
3. Babylon
4. Baton Rouge, Louisiana
5. Boston, Massachusetts
6. Bucharest
7. Cairo
8. Canton, New York
9. Ch'ang-Sha
10. Chicago, Illinois
11. Congo River
12. The Cyclades
13. Decatur, Illinois
14. Fargo, North Dakota
15. Florence
16. Gizeh
17. Granada
18. Hacilar
19. Jerusalem
20. Leopoldville
21. London
22. Los Angeles, California
23. Lung Mên Caves
24. Luxor
25. Malaga
26. Milwaukee, Wisconsin
27. Mississippi River
28. Moscow
29. Mysore Region
30. New Delhi
31. New York, New York
32. Nile River
33. Nimrud
34. Northwest Indians
35. Nuremberg
36. Paris
37. Peking
38. Philadelphia, Pennsylvania
39. Pittsburgh, Pennsylvania
40. Punjab
41. Rockport, Massachusetts
42. Rome
43. Salem, Massachusetts
44. Island of Samothrace
45. Seville
46. Sicily
47. Sippar
48. Stockholm
49. Syracuse
50. Taranto
51. Tell el Amarna
52. Thebes
53. Tokyo
54. Troy
55. Tulum
56. Veracruz
57. Washington, D.C.
58. Woodstock, Vermont

Points of interest in *Looking at Sculpture*

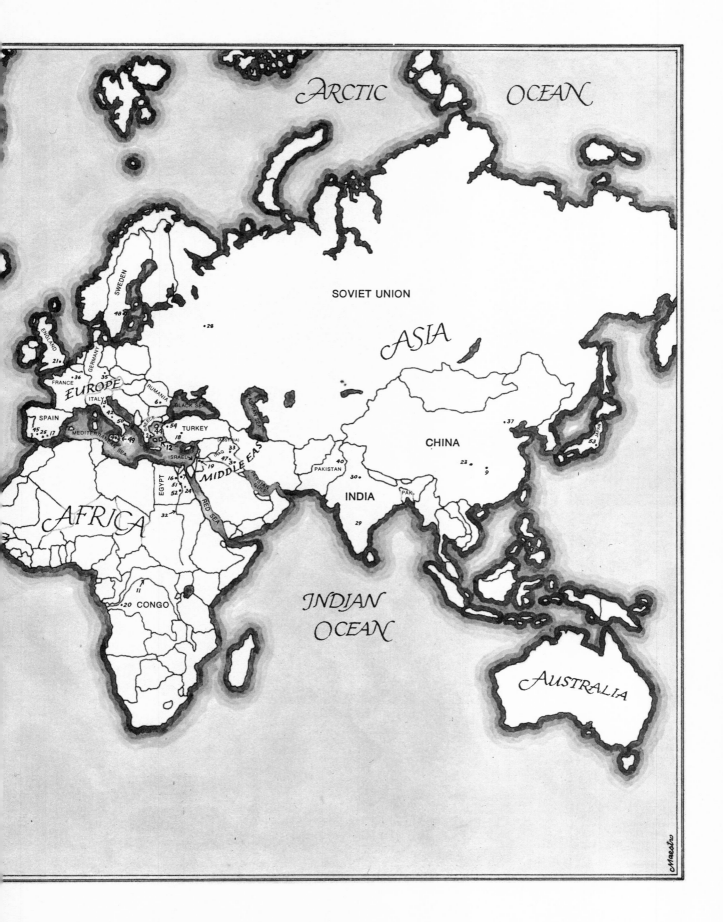

Mallet and Chisel, marble relief made as a shop sign or votive offering, ancient Greek or Roman period, 14 inches high x 11¼ inches wide. *The Metropolitan Museum of Art, Rogers Fund, 1923*

Notes
on the Sculptors

BOCCIONI, UMBERTO (1882-1916) was born in Italy. He helped to found the art style called *futurism*. Futurist artists, both painters and sculptors, were deeply interested in motion and movement. They produced works of art based on natural forms, but done in the abstract with one form moving into and around another. Unique Forms of Continuity in Space (page 71) is a bold design that perfectly expresses the ideas of futurism.

BRANCUSI, CONSTANTIN (1876-1957) was born in Rumania. In 1904 he settled in Paris, where he lived and worked for the rest of his life. Brancusi was one of the most completely abstract and original sculptors of the early twentieth century. He was greatly impressed by African sculpture and art which concentrated on one simple geometric shape for its design. See the Brancusi head and compare it with the African mask on page 19.

CALDER, ALEXANDER (1898-   ) was born, the son of a sculptor, in Philadelphia, Pennsylvania. Calder graduated from Stevens Institute of Technology, Hoboken, New Jersey, and practiced engineering before he turned to sculpture. Calder introduced *kinetics*, or movement, into sculpture when he invented the mobile (page 74). He also introduced the form of sculpture called *stabiles;* the abstract designs are welded together, which makes them "stable," and they stand on the ground rather than hang in space.

DEGAS, EDGAR (1834-1917) was born in Paris, France, the son of a wealthy family. He did not enter his family's business, but instead studied art and became one of the most important of the French 19th century painters. He is best remembered for his pictures about the theatre and ballet and his portraits and scenes depicting horse-races and working people. Throughout his life, however, Degas worked in clay and wax as well as with paints. He created sculptures that are extraordinary studies of movement of the human body. The dancer on page 20 is one of seventy-four figures Degas modeled in wax, which were cast in bronze after his death.

DUCHAMP-VILLON, RAYMOND (1876-1918) was born in France and died at the end of World War I from the effects of poison gas. Though he died young, he left some of the finest twentieth-century sculpture. The Horse (page 15) is considered his masterpiece. In this figure he fused the form of a horse with the shape of a machine to create an image of power.

FLANNAGAN, JOHN BERNARD (1895-1942) was born in Fargo, North Dakota. He studied at the Minneapolis Institute of Fine Arts. Flannagan wrote down some of his ideas in letters to friends. In one he said, "My aim is to produce sculpture as direct and swift as drawing—sculpture with such ease, freedom, and simplicity that it hardly seems carved but rather to have endured so always. This accounts for my preference for field stone; its very rudeness seems to me more in harmony with simple direct statement . . . most often the design dictates the choice of the stone." This sums up the quality of Figure of Dignity on page 13.

FULLER, SUE (1914-   ) was born in Pittsburgh, Pennsylvania, and studied at the Carnegie Institute of Technology. Miss Fuller is an abstract artist and a constructionist. Her original and fascinating designs are splendid *constructions* (page 80).

GROSS, CHAIM (1904-   ) was born in Wolowa, Austria, and is now an American. He studied at the Art Students League in New York. Gross has carved many fine circus sculptures. Lillian Leitzel (page 48) was a famous acrobat. Gross often works in ebony, a wood as hard as stone.

HOUDON, JEAN-ANTOINE (1741-1828) was born in France. He is best remembered for his portrait heads and portrait busts of famous people. In 1785 he visited America and stayed with George Washington at Mt. Vernon. He did portraits of Washington, Lafayette, John Paul Jones, and Thomas Jefferson, as well as Benjamin Franklin (page 10). The bust of Franklin was done in Paris when he was serving as American Ambassador to the court of Louis XVI.

LEONARDO DA VINCI (1452-1519) was born in Italy, and is one of the most famous of Italian painters. In his paintings Mona Lisa and The Last Supper, he revolutionized the methods of showing depth in a picture and character in a portrait. The Horse on page 14 is from a design by Leonardo. Leonardo sketched a plan for a large equestrian sculpture that was never finished. The bronze was cast from the sketch after the artist's death.

LIPPOLD, RICHARD (1915-   ) was born in Milwaukee, Wisconsin. He studied at the Art Institute of Chicago and the University of Chicago. He is one of the leading constructionists. The Metropolitan Museum of Art commissioned him to make The Sun (page 78) in 1953. His work is displayed in many museums and public buildings.

MCINTIRE, SAMUEL (1757-1811) was a wood carver and designer of Salem, Massachusetts. McIntire worked for the wealthy shipowners as architect, builder, and sculptor. It is known that he carved portrait heads, statues, and figureheads from wood, and it is quite probable that he did make the figurehead on page 53.

MICHELANGELO BUONARROTI (1475-1564) was born in Italy and received his first art training in the workshop of the painter Ghirlandaio. In 1489 he studied at an academy of sculpture in Florence and was a frequent student-guest at the palace of Lorenzo de' Medici, the rich and powerful Prince. In the Medici Palace there was a fine collection of ancient sculpture that was of great interest to Michelangelo.

Some of Michelangelo's important sculpture is: Moses (page 39), David, Bound Slaves, Figures for the Medici Tombs. His most important and famous paintings are the frescoes on the walls and ceiling of the Sistine Chapel in the Vatican.

MILLES, CARL (1875-1955) was born at Lagga, Sweden. His art training began in 1892 when he was apprenticed to a cabinet-maker in Stockholm. Later he worked as a sculptor in Paris and assisted in Rodin's studio. In 1931 he moved to the United States and became a citizen in 1945. Some of his best work is fountains. In 1949 he was commissioned by The Metropolitan Museum of Art to design a fountain. In the picture on page 54 you can see Milles at work on the clay models from which the bronze figures were cast for the Aganippe Fountain.

MOORE, HENRY (1898-   ) was born in England and is today one of the most influential and important of contemporary sculptors. He is equally at home working in wood, stone, or clay. Moore has developed several themes in his work, by doing series of The Mother and Child, Family (page 70), The Reclining Figure, and Abstract, Pure Design.

NANNI DI BANCO (c. 1384-1421) was a sculptor of Florence, Italy. He was an early Renaissance artist who worked on the Cathedral of Florence during 1406-7 and later, in 1408, on the Church of Or San Michele. Twelve guilds of the city cooperated in paying for the decoration of the church. Nanni sculptured a life-size figure of Isaiah. Also represented on the church are scenes of the crafts and arts of the twelve guilds. Nanni's scene of sculptors and stonecutters is illustrated on page 82.

NOGUCHI, ISAMU (1904-   ) was born in Los Angeles, California. He spent his childhood in Japan and returned to the United States in 1918. Noguchi planned on being a doctor, but after two years of medicine he gave it up and devoted himself to sculpture. As a young student, he went to Paris and, in 1927-28, worked as an assistant to Brancusi. The stark, bonelike figure Kouros (page 43) is typical of Noguchi's style. He also designs "sculpture gardens." One is the garden of the UNESCO Headquarters in Paris; another is the Billy Rose Sculpture Garden at the Israel Museum, Jerusalem.

PICASSO, PABLO (1881-   ) is the most influential artist of the twentieth century; he is a painter, ceramic designer, printmaker, and sculptor. Picasso was born in Malaga, Spain, but has spent most of his life in France. In Paris, during the years 1909-12, he started a new style of art with the painter Georges Braque. It is called *cubism*. Head of a Woman (page 18) is an example of cubism in sculpture.

PISANO, ANDREA (c. 1290-1348) was an Italian sculptor. Very little is known about his life before 1330, when he came to Florence to design and make a pair of bronze doors for the Baptistry. After 1337, the year the painter Giotto died, Pisano was appointed chief of construction and decoration of the Campanile (Bell Tower), the position held by Giotto. The Campanile is decorated with relief sculpture by Pisano representing the arts and crafts. Sculpture on page 22 is part of the series.

POWERS, HIRAM (1805-73) was born in Woodstock, Vermont, and died in Florence, Italy, where he worked most of his life. In 1835 he went to Washington, D. C., to model the portrait of President Andrew Jackson (page 17). He carried out the President's wishes on how he wished to look. There is a record of their conversation. The President said, "Make me as I am, Mr. Powers, and be true to nature always. I have no desire to look young as long as I feel old." Powers took his original work in clay to Florence, and there he cut it in marble.

REMINGTON, FREDERIC (1861-1909) was born in Canton, New York. He studied at the Yale University Art School for one year and then went West. He worked as a ranch cook and cowboy for several years. When he returned home he had hundreds of drawings of life and people of the Western ranges. His paintings and sculpture like Comin' Through the Rye (page 116) are based on these firsthand drawings and his memory of cowboys.

DE RIVERA, JOSÉ (1904-   ) was born near Baton Rouge, Louisiana. He studied painting and drawing in Chicago, and later turned to sculpture. Rivera has devoted himself to an abstract style. His design, Homage to the World of Minkowski (page 11), honors the theory of a Russian mathematician, who was the first to state that time and space could not be understood separately. This concept is the basis for Einstein's Theory of Relativity. There is a motor in the base of the sculpture, which turns the design in space at a constant rate of speed.

DELLA ROBBIA, ANDREA (1435-1525) was the nephew and chief pupil of Luca della Robbia, who maintained and ran a workshop in Florence, Italy. The della Robbias were a family of sculptors who worked in marble and bronze, but are most often remembered for their terra-cotta sculpture. They devised an ingenious glaze for clay which, when fired, made a very hard and glassy surface. Andrea is the artist who modeled the series of Bambini (babies) for the wall of the Foundling Home in Florence. The swaddled babies, like St. Michael on page 88, are sculpture in relief, made to decorate a building.

RODIN, AUGUSTE (1840-1917) was born in Paris, France. He began his art study when he was fourteen, and at the same time earned a living as a stonecutter. He visited Italy and was greatly impressed by all he saw, particularly the Moses by Michelangelo. He is the most important of late nineteenth-century sculptors. His style is described as *impressionistic,* as his life and art parallel the period and manner of the French impressionist painters. He was as interested in the contrast of light and dark on the surfaces of marble, clay, or bronze as the painters were in new ways to picture light.

SMITH, DAVID (1906-65) was born in Decatur, Illinois. Smith studied at Ohio University and the Art Students League in New York. His sculpture is abstract, large and, most often, welded. His designs like Tanktotem (page 77) are contemporary in their materials and technique. Smith often created figures as symbols.

VISCHER, PETER (c. 1455-1529) was born in Germany and maintained one of the most famous bronze-casting foundries at Nuremberg. Orders for casting came from all over Europe. Vischer's masterpiece in bronze is the Shrine of Saint Sebald in the Cathedral at Nuremberg. Vischer included a portrait of his father, page 62, among the figures on the shrine.

School Exercise Tablet with cuneiform letters, clay, from the temple school at Sippar, Iraq, about 2100 B.C. *The Metropolitan Museum of Art, Funds from various donors, 1886*

Glossary

Adze: an axe-like tool used for roughing out wood sculpture.

Drawing of a wall relief in the Tomb of Ti at Sakkara, Egypt. (ca. 2750-2625 B.C.)

Alabaster: a translucent stone of two types: one is a variety of gypsum; the other a pure white calcite.

Alloy: a metal formed from mixing two or more metals, as bronze, brass, chrome steel.

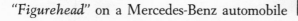

"Figurehead" on a Mercedes-Benz automobile

Anatomy: the make-up and structure of a body; the science of the structure of a body.

The Academy (detail), engraving after Stradanus by Cort, 1578, Netherlands. *The Metropolitan Museum of Art, Harris Brisbane Dick Fund, 1953*

Antefix: an ornamental figure to disguise the joints of a roof.

Aquamanile: (from Latin, *aqua,* water; *manus,* hand) a water container used for washing the hands in church rituals. During the Middle Ages also used in castles for washing the hands during meals.

Armature: a framework for modeling; resembles a stick figure skeleton and may be constructed from wire, wood, or metal pipes.

Bronze: an alloy of copper and tin, sometimes with other metals added, as lead and zinc. The principal metal for cast sculpture.

Bronze Age: a period to describe man's stage of civilization. It follows the Stone Age and precedes the Iron Age. Bronze appears to have been first made in parts of Europe by 3000 B.C.

Bronzing: the application of an imitation bronze finish to a sculpture made of another material so that it will look like bronze.

Cabinetmaker: a skilled craftsman and artist who designs and carves furniture and wood paneling.

Chair—Chippendale Style (detail: foot), 1760-1770, American. *The Metropolitan Museum of Art, Gift of Mrs. George Sands Bryan in memory of her husband George Sands Bryan, 1946*

Carve, Carving: in sculpture, to cut wood or stone in an artistic way.

Caryatid: a statue of a female figure used in place of a column to support a building.

Cast: to form a shape by pouring a liquid material into a mold. Also the figure which has been formed in the mold is a cast or casting.

Ceramics: a term to describe all objects made from clay.

Chisel: a metal tool with the cutting edge at the end of the blade; a chisel may be toothed or flat-edged.

Cire Perdue: French for lost wax *(see)*.

Claw: a toothed-edged chisel.

Clay: that type of earth which can be modeled; clay deposits are found throughout the world in a variety of grades and colors. (*See* Porcelain)

Colossal: (from Latin, *colossus,* gigantic) a statue of huge size, at least twice life-size.

Commission: in art, the order for a work of art. The one who commissions a work of art is called the patron.

Composition: For an artist, it is the use and placement of shapes, lines, and color that make a harmonious and meaningful arrangement, a design. For a writer, it is the selection and placement of words, sentences, paragraphs. Each art form, music, painting, sculpture, writing, dance, has composition.

Construction: in sculpture, the assembling and joining of pieces of material to make a design. The 20th-century sculptors who make constructions are called constructionists or constructivists.

Diorite: a very hard stone; a type of igneous rock. This type of rock was formed by molten material in the earth cooling and crystallizing.

Diptych: (from Greek, folded) a folding picture used as an altarpiece or small shrine; in ancient times a diptych was a two-part writing tablet.

·113·

Direct Method: describes the procedure of a sculptor who cuts directly into his material, particularly wood or stone. It also applies to modeling or beating designs in metal. (*See* Indirect Method)

Dowel: a wooden or metallic pin used to join pieces of wood or metal together.

Earthenware: objects made from clay and fired in a kiln; the coarsest variety of clay.

Ebony: a very hard and durable wood from trees that grow in tropical regions.

Effigy: a likeness of a person; a tomb effigy is the figure and likeness of a person sculptured on his grave monument.

Façade: the face, front side of a building.

Customs House, 1818, Salem, Massachusetts

Facet: one of many small surfaces or planes like the facets on a diamond. Picasso modeled the Head of a Woman as if it were faceted (page 18).

Figurine: a small carved or modeled figure or group; it can be used interchangeably with statuette (*see*) but figurine is usually used to describe sculpture that is more ornamental than important in its subject matter.

Finishes: the special surface treatments for sculpture. (*See* Patina)

Firing: in ceramics, the action of heating a kiln (oven) to bake, or fire, clay; the firing of the clay to make it hard and permanent.

Flutes: the vertical grooves on the shaft of a column; other carving or decoration that resembles the surface of a column is said to be fluted or to have fluting.

·114·

Fluted Columns, Town House,
New York City, 20th century

Foundry: (from Latin, *fundere,* to found or pour) the workshop where casting is done.

Fountain Sculpture: sculpture which is not only used to decorate a fountain or well, but is often also a part of its water system.

Fountain of the Lions (detail), The Alhambra, Granada, Spain, 14th century Moorish stone sculpture

Freestanding: describes a figure or a column that is not attached to a wall or background. It can be used interchangeably with "sculpture in the round" when the sculpture is literally *standing* resting on a plinth *(see)* or pedestal or ground. For example, a mobile is "in the round" but it is not freestanding.

Frieze: that kind of relief sculpture which is a long horizontal band and usually applied to the wall of a building.

Animal Relief,
Central Park Zoo,
New York City

Frontal: in sculpture, a figure posed so that there is no movement to either side; one where a vertical line drawn down the middle of the figure would divide it in exactly equal halves.

Gudea, Sumerian ruler, from Lagash, ca. 2150 B.C., diorite, 17-5/16 inches high. *The Metropolitan Museum of Art, Harris Brisbane Dick Fund, 1959*

Furnace: in a foundry a large structure that can be heated to many thousand degrees and thereby reduce bronze to a molten state.

·115·

Gilt, Gilding: a finish, particularly for wood sculpture but also used on bronze; thin leaves of gold are burnished onto the surface with a special adhesive.

Glazes: the special pigments or colors used to paint pottery, which, because they are made from the same basic materials as glass, melt, fuse, and harden when fired at a high temperature. Glazes decorate and protect objects made from clay.

Gouge: a kind of chisel with a curved blade, like a scoop, used for carving wood sculpture.

Granite: a very hard igneous rock (*see* Diorite) used for sculpture and building. It is so hard and enduring that granite is used to describe anything hard and long lasting.

Granite Quarries at Rockport, Massachusetts

Group: in sculpture, a design that includes two or more figures.

Comin' Through the Rye by Frederic Remington, 1902, bronze, *The Metropolitan Museum of Art, Bequest of Jacob Rupert, 1939*

Gypsum: a mineral substance, mined and used to make plaster of Paris (*see*).

Hammer, Hammered: a hammer is the tool with a metal head used for breaking stones and hammering metals in sculpture. Metals that have designs beaten into their surfaces are said to be hammered. (*See* Mallet)

Incise: to cut into a solid surface.

Indirect Method: particularly the practice of sculptors who make either a small or full-size model of their design (most often in clay, wax, or plaster of Paris) and then turn it over to professional stonecutters or assistants to enlarge and carve in stone. The transfer of the original model to its permanent form is done mathematically by a pointing machine.

Ideal Art: the art of a culture or country that represents the highest standard of beauty and perfection. The ancient Greeks conceived the Ideal as one based on perfect human proportions. Usually all that is uneven, ugly, or defacing that can be seen in people is omitted.

Intaglio: the cutting and incising of designs into the surface of a solid material, most often stone or gem stones.

Ivory: the tusks of elephants; also the tusks of walrus and wild boar. Substitutes for ivory can be the bones of animals.

Join, Joiner: to fasten two pieces of material together with dowels and/or glue. A joiner is a craftsman who works in wood and is not of the artistic status of a cabinetmaker or wood sculptor.

Woodcarver's Workshop, 18th-century French engraving from Diderot *Encyclopedie ou dictionaire raisonné des sciences* in The Metropolitan Museum of Art.

Kiln: a special oven for the firing and glazing of ceramics.

Life-Size: equal to life in all proportions as well as size.

Limestone: a plentiful stone used for sculpture and building; crystalline limestone is marble. Limestone is a rock consisting mainly of calcium carbonate, and an accumulation of the remains of natural matter like shells. It is not as hard as the igneous rocks like granite and diorite.

·II7·

Lost Wax Process: (in French called *cire perdue*) the method invented in ancient times for casting sculpture from bronze as well as gold and silver.

Mallet: a hammer with a wooden head used for driving or hitting a chisel or gouge.

Miniature: in sculpture a figure or ornament on a *very* small scale.

Miniature Tragic Mask With Onkos, terra-cotta, from Tarentum, Greek, IV? century. *The Metropolitan Museum of Art, Rogers Fund, 1910*

Mobile: art term for a type of sculpture that moves.

Model: to work clay or wax or other soft, pliable material with the fingers or modeling tools. Also, the sketch or design for sculpture to be made in larger size or other material.

Modeling Tools: most important are the fingers; but modelers also use knives, wire-loop tools, spatulas.

Molten: melted at a very high temperature so that a substance is molten, in a liquid, runny state.

Monument: in sculpture, a statue or figure erected to remind us of a person or event.

Fishermen Monument, Gloucester, Massachusetts

Niche: a space, a recess in a wall to hold a statue.

Nike: (pronounce, Knee-Kay) Greek word for Victory, as Nike of Samothrace. A goddess-like figure with wings.

Offering: a special gift to one's church, god, or gods. When given with special vows or promises, it may be a votive *(see)* offering.

Patina: a surface film that forms on copper or bronze after long exposure to the air, a "green patina." Patination is a type of special finish that can be given to sculpture. An artificial patina can be made by applying paint or chemicals.

Patron: in art, the customer, the supporter of an artist; one who commissions works of art.

Plane: a flat surface on which if any two points are taken the straight line that joins the points is wholly on that surface.

Plaster, Plaster of Paris: a pasty material made from lime, water, and sand and used in sculpture as a modeling material. The finer-grade plaster most used by artists is plaster of Paris, which also includes fine-grain gypsum. Unlike clay, which must be fired to properly harden it, plasters harden and set without heating.

Plinth: the block that serves as a base for a statue.

Point: a simple, pointed tool made of iron, bronze, or steel for roughing out a stone sculpture.

Pointing, Pointing Machine: a mechanical means for transferring a sculptor's original work into stone. Points are placed at different distances on the model. These points are often nailheads. The identical marks and measurements are put on a block of stone. The stonecutter carves the shapes and forms as they appear between the points, copying the original. This is a system and equipment for the Indirect Method.

Polishers: a variety of tools used for giving a sculpture in wood or stone its final surface. Polishing stones and abrasives like sand are used on stone; sandpaper and steel wool on wood; burnishers with emery and pumice on metals.

Porcelain: the special high-grade type of clay called kaolin. The dishes and sculpture described as porcelain are made from kaolin or clay that resembles kaolin.

Portrait Head, Portrait Bust: both are lifelike representations of a person; one is only the head and neck; the other includes the shoulders and sometimes the chest of the person.

Marie of France, marble by Jean de Liège, ca. 1382, French, *The Metropolitan Museum of Art, Gift of George Blumenthal, 1941*

Pottery: things made from clay other than porcelain.

Pumice: a polishing material made from lava rock.

Rasp: a coarse metal file with sharp triangular teeth used in wood sculpture.

Relief: the term in sculpture for designs carved or modeled on a flat surface and still attached to or cut into a surface. Relief may be sunk (below surface), low (project somewhat above surface), or high (project more). The term *bas relief* is French, meaning low relief; it is a term used in English.

Repoussé: (French for thrown back) the work and the final design on metal made by hammering a pattern from the reverse side.

Rifflers: tools with curved blades and rough surfaces, like a file, which are used on stone, wood, and plaster of Paris figures.

Sandstone: a soft stone consisting of sand, usually some quartz, and some silica. There are several varieties and colors of sandstone.

Statuary: a collection of statues.

Statue: the image of a person or figure in the round.

Statuette: a little statue; usually between 5 and 20 inches high; a word that suggests a more important subject than figurine. Statuettes include figures of ancient gods, goddesses, kings, as well as holy figures for churches.

Stele: (Greek for a post or marker) a slab or pillar of stone used as a special marker, particularly as a monument or grave stone.

Stonecutter, Stonemason: craftsmen who cut and dress stone for building and act as assistants to a sculptor.

Terra-Cotta: (Italian, *terra* is earth; *cotta* is cooked) "cooked earth" is this variety of clay which is brown, yellow, or orange in color when it is baked or fired. It is often used for relief sculpture and colored with glazes.

Terra-cotta Cock (Bucchero ware),
Etruscan with incised alphabet, 4-1/16 inches high.
7th century B.C., *The Metropolitan Museum of Art, Fletcher Fund, 1924*

Translucent: partly transparent, shining, glowing as a translucent piece of marble or alabaster.

Volume: in geometry the space or the solid mass contained or enclosed by planes.

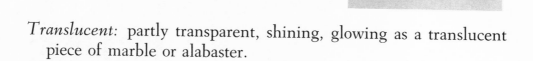

Votive: given with a vow or a prayer or in fulfillment of a prayer, as a votive offering. A votary is one who makes the offering.

Wax: an ancient and still most important modeling material. The basic material for modeling figures to be cast in bronze or other metals.

·121·

Welding: the joining of pieces of metal by heating the surfaces of their edges so that they melt and fuse together. The acetylene torch is the modern tool for welding and is used by sculptors.

Detail of decorative ironwork

Wood: a primary, most important material for sculpture. Wood falls into two general types: Hardwoods are those from deciduous trees, like oak, maple, birch, that lose their leaves in the winter. Softwoods are those from coniferous trees, like pine, hemlock, spruce, which bear cones and do not drop their foliage.

Workshop: the place of work and business for an artist, particularly from ancient times until the 17th or 18th century. In a workshop, a master artist employed assistants, trained apprentices in his trade, craft, or art. The workshop system has mostly disappeared in modern times and has been replaced by studios, private workrooms where artists work alone.

·I22·

Hiram Powers' Studio in Florence, from *Harpers' Weekly,* photo, *The Metropolitan Museum of Art*

The Education of the Virgin, sandstone group, French, early 16th century, 57¼ inches high. The young Mary with her mother Saint Anne. *The Metropolitan Museum of Art, Gift of J. Pierpont Morgan, 1916*

Books
For Further Reading

Johnson, Lillian, *The Basic Methods and Materials of Sculpture.* New York, David McKay Co., 1960.

Ripley, Elizabeth, *Michelangelo.* New York, Henry Z. Walck, 1953.

Ripley, Elizabeth, *Rodin.* Philadelphia, J. B. Lippincott, 1966.

Slade, Richard, *Modeling in Clay, Plaster, and Papier-Mâché.* New York, Lothrop, Lee & Shepard Co., 1968.

More Advanced Books

Gombrich, E. H., *The Story of Art.* New York, Phaidon Art Books, 1958. (In paper: Oxford University Press, New York, 1966.) A complete survey of the arts, gracefully and accurately written for those interested in reading and seeing sculpture in conjunction with painting and architecture.

Mills, John, *The Technique of Sculpture.* New York, Reinhold Publishing Corp., 1965. An excellent description of the techniques and attitudes of an artist. Mills is a contemporary British sculptor.

Read, Herbert, *The Art of Sculpture.* Princeton, N. J., Princeton University Press, 1961.

Terra-cotta Cock (Bucchero ware), Etruscan wtih incised alphabet, 7th century
B.C., 4⅟₁₆ inches high. *The Metropolitan Museum of Art, Fletcher Fund, 1924*

Index to Sculpture

(For sculptors, see *Notes on the Sculptors*. For technical terms, see *Glossary*.)

A

Animal relief (American), 115
Archangel Saint Michael by della
    Robbia, 88
Armor (German), 73
Assembly Room (American), 91
Athena Flying Her Owl (Greek), 64
"Atlas" by Michelangelo, 38

B

Benjamin Franklin by Houdon, 10
Benjamin Franklin and King Louis
    XVI (French), 58
Boat, Ancient Model of, (Egyptian),
    47

C

Chippendale-chair detail
    (American), 112
Cock, Terra-cotta, (Etruscan), 121,
    126
Coins (Greek and American), 86
Columns, Fluted, (American), 114
Comin' Through the Rye by
    Remington, 116
Customs House (American), 114

D

Diadem, Gold, (Greek), 94
Diptych, Ivory, (French), 95

E

Eagle, American, 10
Education of the Virgin, The,
    (French), 124

F

Family Group by Moore, 70
Female Statuette (from Hacilar), 55
"Figurehead" (automobile), 111
Figurehead (American), 53
Figurehead and Bow (American), 53
Figure of Dignity—Irish Mountain
    Goat by Flannagan, 13
Fishermen Monument (American),
    118

G

Gorgon Face, 89
Guardian Figure (Mexican), 40
Gudea (Sumerian), 9, 115

H

Harp Player (Cycladic), 31
Harpsichord (Italian), 52
Head of a Woman by Picasso, 18
Helmet (Greek), 63
Homage to the World of Minkowski
    by de Rivera, 11
Horse (Chinese), 57
Horse (Greek), 14
Horse, The, by Duchamp-Villon, 15
Horse, Rearing, by da Vinci, 14
Horse-Shaped Aquamanile (German),
    15
Horse-Shaped Whip Handle
    (Egyptian), 15

I

Ironwork (American), 122

J

Jaina Temple, Carved Wall from,
    (Indian), 90

·127·

K

King Akhenaten (Egyptian), 85
King Amenophis III (Egyptian), 25
Knight, Effigy of, (French), 97
Kouros by Noguchi, 43
Kuan Yin (Chinese), 50

L

Laocoön and His Sons
    (Greek), 36
Lillian Leitzel by Gross, 48
Lion, Striding, (Babylonian), 2–3, 87
Lion, Winged, (Assyrian), 93
Lions, Fountain of (Spain—Moorish),
    115

M

Maidens on the Porch of the
    Erectheum (Greek), 33, 34
Mallet and Chisel (Greek or
    Roman), 102
Marie of France by de Liège, 120
Mask (African), 19
Mask, Tragic, (Greek), 118
Moses by Michelangelo, 1, 39
Mummy Case for a Cat (Egyptian),
    11
Mummy Cases (Egyptian), 45

O

Ox and Cart (Chinese), 56

P

Peter Vischer, The Elder, by
    Peter Vischer, 5, 62
President Andrew Jackson by Powers,
    17
Princess Meryetaten (Egyptian), 16
Procession of the Emperor and His
    Courtiers (Chinese), 84

Q

Quail Chicks (Egyptian), 13
Queen Hatshepsut (Egyptian), 26

R

Rattle (Northwest American
    Indian), 52
Red Gongs by Calder, 74
Royal Head, Sculptor's Model of,
    (Egyptian), 29

S

School Exercise Tablet (from
    Iraq), 110
Sculptor Carving a Corinthian Capital
    (French), 44
Sculptor Carving a Statue by Pisano,
    23
Sculptors and Stonecutters by
    di Banco, 82
Sleeping Muse by Brancusi, 19
Spanish Dance, The, by Degas, 20
Stamp Seal (Indian), 85
String Composition No. 50 by
    Fuller, 80
Sun, The (Variation Within a
    Sphere, No. 10) by Lippold, 78

T

Tanktotem II by Smith, 77
Thinker, The, by Rodin, 68
Tomb Figure (Chinese), 49
Tombstone (American), 96
Town Hall (Spanish), 92
Triton and Nereid by Rodin, 59

U

Unique Forms of Continuity in
Space by Boccioni, 71

V

Victory of Samothrace (Greek), 35
Virgin and Child (French), 51
Vishnu (Indian), 84

W

Warrior, Greek, 99